Would You Rather
Book for Teenagers
by Shut Up Coloring

WOULD YOU RATHER...

share your room with your sibling   move into the attic?

 or

WOULD YOU RATHER WEAR...

a uniform to school   casual outfits to school?

 or

WOULD YOU RATHER WEAR...

sneakers to school

shoes to school?

or

WOULD YOU RATHER BE A FAST...

writer

reader?

or

WOULD YOU RATHER LISTEN TO MUSIC WITH...

headphones

earphones?

or

WOULD YOU RATHER SPEND THE WEEKEND...

indoors

outdoors?

or

WOULD YOU RATHER GO TO...

a picnic   a cook-out?

or

WOULD YOU RATHER GO TO...

a pool party   a beach party?

or

WOULD YOU RATHER...

jog around

take a stroll?

or

WOULD YOU RATHER TRAVEL...

by road

by air?

or

WOULD YOU RATHER HAVE...

your own car   your own house?

or

WOULD YOU RATHER HAVE...

your phone taken away   your laptop taken away?

or

WOULD YOU RATHER IT WAS...

winter all the time   it was summer all the time?

 or

WOULD YOU RATHER HAVE...

blue eyes   brown eyes?

 or

WOULD YOU RATHER...

curl your hair

dye your hair?

or

WOULD YOU RATHER VISIT...

a museum

an art gallery?

or

WOULD YOU RATHER HAVE...

a big bed

a big bedroom?

or

WOULD YOU RATHER WEAR...

leather clothing

cotton clothing?

or

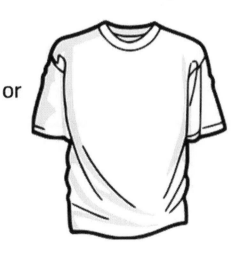

WOULD YOU RATHER HAVE...

a pool a jacuzzi?

 or

WOULD YOU RATHER...

cook dinner   wash the dishes after dinner?

 or

WOULD YOU RATHER ACT...

as the villain in a movie

be the hero?

or

WOULD YOU RATHER MEET...

a famous movie star

a famous musician?

or

WOULD YOU RATHER SURF...

the internet   the ocean?

   or

---

WOULD YOU RATHER BE OUT WHEN...

it's raining   it's really sunny?

   or

WOULD YOU RATHER GET...

chocolates   candies?

   or

WOULD YOU RATHER HAVE...

a maid   a chef?

   or

WOULD YOU RATHER TAKE...

a shower

a bath?

or

WOULD YOU RATHER EAT...

a cake

a pie?

or

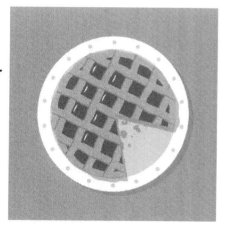

WOULD YOU RATHER WORK PART-TIME AT...

a clothing store

a bookstore?

or

WOULD YOU RATHER USE...

an iPhone

a Samsung?

or

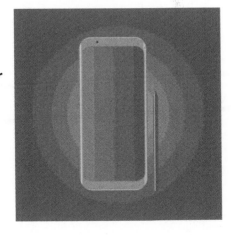

WOULD YOU RATHER EAT...

in bed

in front of the TV?

or

WOULD YOU RATHER...

eat a bowl of ice-cream

drink a cup of hot chocolate?

or

WOULD YOU RATHER HAVE...

a skateboard   a hover-board?

or

WOULD YOU RATHER WIN...

a sports car   a bike?

or

WOULD YOU RATHER BE...

really tall

really short?

or

WOULD YOU RATHER RIDE ON...

a horse's back

a camel's back?

or

WOULD YOU RATHER BE IN...

a quiz competition

debate competition?

or

WOULD YOU RATHER EAT ONLY...

vegetables for a month

fruits for a month?

or

WOULD YOU RATHER DRINK...

tea   orange juice during breakfast?

or

WOULD YOU RATHER KNOW HOW TO PLAY...

the piano   the guitar?

or

WOULD YOU RATHER GO...

fishing

hunting?

or

WOULD YOU RATHER KNOW HOW TO...

swim

surf?

or

WOULD YOU RATHER DRESS...

fashionably   comfortably?

or

WOULD YOU RATHER...

win a gift card   win cash?

or

WOULD YOU RATHER HAVE...

really large feet

really large hands?

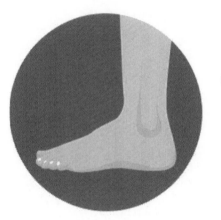

or

WOULD YOU RATHER...

constantly sneeze

constantly itch?

or

WOULD YOU RATHER HAVE...

a monkey that talks

a monkey that dances?

or

WOULD YOU RATHER HAVE...

all your teeth fall out

all your hair fall out?

or

WOULD YOU RATHER...

hop around

walk backward?

or

WOULD YOU RATHER...

kiss a frog

hug a skunk?

or

WOULD YOU RATHER HAVE...

all your teeth fall out

two tongues?

or

WOULD YOU RATHER...

be really hairy all over

have a bald head?

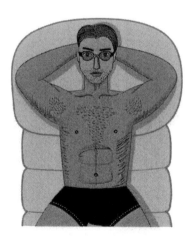

or

WOULD YOU RATHER HAVE...

a big head

a long neck?

or

WOULD YOU RATHER...

be in college already

go back to Kindergarten?

or

WOULD YOU RATHER SIT ON...

something wet

something sticky?

or

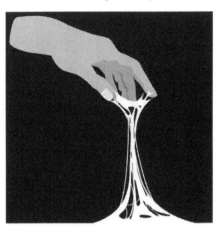

WOULD YOU RATHER...

have wings

have a tail?

or

WOULD YOU RATHER BE ABDUCTED BY...

Zombies

Aliens?

or

WOULD YOU RATHER...

fall asleep for a year

have insomnia for a year?

or

WOULD YOU RATHER HAVE...

a fat tummy

fat cheeks?

or

WOULD YOU RATHER...

fall off a bike

fall off a skateboard?

or

WOULD YOU RATHER BE...

terrible at cooking   terrible at baking?

or

WOULD YOU RATHER...

fall into a swimming pool   fall into a pool of water?

or

WOULD YOU RATHER...

work as a clown   work in a circus?

 or

WOULD YOU RATHER...

chase a crawling cockroach   be chased by a flying cockroach?

 or

WOULD YOU RATHER BE...

pursued by chickens

pursued by turkeys?

or

WOULD YOU RATHER SIT IN BETWEEN ...

two really fat people

two really smelly people?

or

WOULD YOU RATHER HAVE TO WORK ON...

a farm after school   a field after school?

   or

WOULD YOU RATHER YOUR PARENTS...

forgot your birthday   forgot your graduation day?

   or

WOULD YOU RATHER...

cheat on a test   fail a test?

or

WOULD YOU RATHER...

delete Snapchat   stop watching Instagram stories?

or

WOULD YOU RATHER FORGET HOW TO...

read

write?

or

WOULD YOU RATHER BE...

home alone after school

with a very annoying relative?

or

WOULD YOU RATHER BE...

freaking cold

super hot?

or

WOULD YOU RATHER HAVE...

a hiccup that refused to go

a cough that refused to go?

or

WOULD YOU RATHER...

climb the highest mountains   swim the deepest seas?

 or

WOULD YOU RATHER...

stay in a coma for 15 years   be in prison for 15 years?

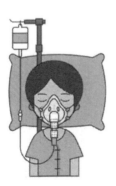 or

WOULD YOU RATHER LIVE WITH JUST...

your dad

your mom?

or

WOULD YOU RATHER...

sky dive

scuba dive?

or

WOULD YOU RATHER GET...

an injection when sick

a lot of drugs when sick?

or

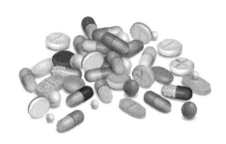

WOULD YOU RATHER DO...

all the cleaning at home

all the cooking?

or

WOULD YOU RATHER LIVE...

in a cave   on an island?

or

WOULD YOU RATHER MOVE TO...

a smaller school   a smaller house?

or

WOULD YOU RATHER LICK...

your socks

the sole of your shoe?

or

WOULD YOU RATHER LET WORMS...

crawl up your nose

crawl into your ears?

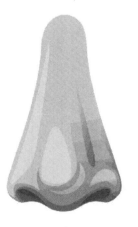

or

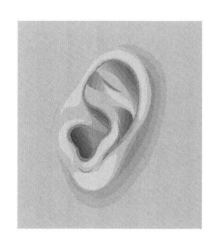

WOULD YOU RATHER...

eat a bar of soap

drink liquid soap?

or

WOULD YOU RATHER EAT...

an eyeball

a toe?

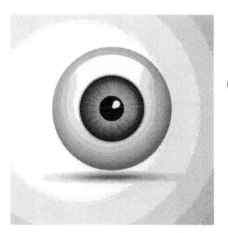

or

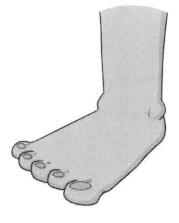

WOULD YOU RATHER ACCIDENTALLY SWALLOW...

a button

a needle?

or

WOULD YOU RATHER DRINK A GALLON OF...

mayonnaise

mustard?

or

WOULD YOU RATHER...

not shower for a week   not shave for a week?

or

WOULD YOU RATHER BE SERVED...

food on a dirty plate   dirty food?

or

WOULD YOU RATHER HAVE...

dandruff in your hair   lice in your hair?

or

WOULD YOU RATHER SUCK ON...

on a goat's beard   on a stranger's beard?

or

WOULD YOU RATHER...

throw up when sick

spit a lot when sick?

or

WOULD YOU RATHER BATHE IN A TUB FULL...

of cockroaches

of bugs?

or

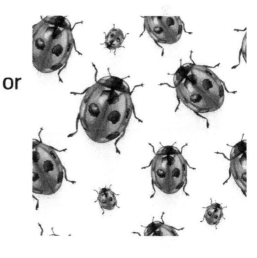

WOULD YOU RATHER EAT...

rotten fish   rotten meat?

or

WOULD YOU RATHER BE...

a fashion designer   a fashion model?

or

WOULD YOU RATHER BE...

a fast writer

a fast reader?

or

WOULD YOU RATHER BE...

a talk show host

a runway model?

or

WOULD YOU RATHER...

be able to wake up early

be able to go to bed early?

or

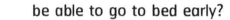

WOULD YOU RATHER...

be alone when sick

have a lot of friends around?

or

WOULD YOU RATHER BE...

an adult already

a child again?

or

WOULD YOU RATHER BE...

an only child

have lots of siblings?

or

WOULD YOU RATHER BE IN...

a ballet class   a salsa class?

   or

WOULD YOU RATHER BE OUT...

when it's raining   when it's really sunny?

   or

WOULD YOU RATHER DO...

cardio   weights?

   or

WOULD YOU RATHER...

do sports   watch sports?

   or

WOULD YOU RATHER DRINK...

hot chocolate

a cold sundae?

or

WOULD YOU RATHER DRINK...

Red wine

white wine?

or

WOULD YOU RATHER DRINK...

smoothies   milkshakes?

   or

WOULD YOU RATHER DRINK...

tea   orange juice during breakfast?

   or

WOULD YOU RATHER EAT...

a cake   a pie?

   or

WOULD YOU RATHER GET...

a free hairdo   a free makeover?

   or